WE THE PEOPLE

The Powhatan
and Their History

By Natalie M. Rosinsky

Content Adviser: Bruce Bernstein, Ph.D.,
Assistant Director for Cultural Resources,
National Museum of the American Indian, Smithsonian Institution

Reading Adviser: Rosemary G. Palmer, Ph.D.,
Department of Literacy, College of Education,
Boise State University

COMPASS POINT BOOKS
MINNEAPOLIS, MINNESOTA

Compass Point Books
3109 West 50th Street, #115
Minneapolis, MN 55410

Visit Compass Point Books on the Internet at *www.compasspointbooks.com*
or e-mail your request to *custserv@compasspointbooks.com*

On the cover: A 1590 hand-colored engraving of a Virginia Native American village and gardens

Photographs ©: North Wind Picture Archives, cover, 8, 13, 17, 20, 21, 23, 32, 33; Prints Old & Rare, back cover (far left); Library of Congress, back cover; Bettmann/Corbis, 4, 5; Peter Harholdt/ Corbis, 6; Marilyn "Angel" Wynn, 7, 9, 11, 15, 16, 18, 19, 22, 24, 27, 35, 37; Photodisc, 26; Getty Images, 29; Kean Collection/Getty Images, 31; Hulton Archive/Getty Images, 34; Rankokus Indian Reservation, 38; AP Photo/Dennis Cook, 39; Gary Meszaros/Dembinsky Photo Associates, 40; Kit Breen, 41; John Cross/The Free Press, 48.

Creative Director: Terri Foley
Managing Editor: Catherine Neitge
Art Director: Keith Griffin
Photo Researcher: Marcie C. Spence
Designer/Page production: Bradfordesign, Inc./Les Tranby
Cartographer: XNR Productions, Inc.
Educational Consultant: Diane Smolinski

Library of Congress Cataloging-in-Publication Data
Rosinsky, Natalie M. (Natalie Myra)
 The Powhatan and their history / by Natalie M. Rosinsky.
    p. cm. — (We the people)
 Includes bibliographical references and index.
  ISBN 0-7565-0844-4 (hardcover)
  1. Powhatan Indians—History—Juvenile literature. 2. Powhatan Indians—Social life and customs—Juvenile literature. I. Title. II. We the people (Series) (Compass Point Books)
E99.P85R655 2005
975.5004'97347—dc22   2004018966

TABLE OF CONTENTS

A LAST-MINUTE RESCUE?

It was late December 1607—the season the Powhatan people call the Time of Long Nights. The last weeks had indeed felt long to one frightened prisoner, Captain John Smith. In what is now Virginia, this English soldier had been captured by Powhatan warriors. They were defending the territory of their great chief, Wahunsanacock, who was

The British colonists acknowledge Wahunsanacock as "king" of the Powhatan.

Captain John Smith

also called Powhatan by the English colonists. Smith and these colonists had arrived just the past May.

As Smith later wrote, he was held captive by "30 or 40 tall fellows" who each day brought him more bread and meat "than would have served 20 men." Smith thought the Powhatan were trying to fatten him up in order to eat him! He refused most of the food, which the guards then ate. Smith was certain he was facing death when the guards and a Powhatan priest—"a great grim fellow, all painted over with coal"—finally took him to meet mighty Wahunsanacock.

When John Smith entered the dark lodge, he saw an old, gray-haired man sitting before a fire. Wahunsanacock was richly dressed in a raccoon skin robe, with many tails

A 17th-century German map of Virginia includes drawings of Powhatan.

still attached. He wore chains of pearls around his neck. His body was strong for his years. He was surrounded by 10 young men and 10 young women. They roared as Smith walked toward their great leader.

While Wahunsanacock questioned him, John Smith noticed that the men carried heavy war clubs. Suddenly, Smith was dragged over to a large stone. He was forced to his knees, and his head was pushed against the stone. Two

men raised their clubs and
prepared to strike! According
to Smith, that is when he was
rescued from death. He later
wrote that a young girl risked
"the beating out of her own
brains" to save his. She was
Matoaka, also called Pocahontas,
one of the chief's daughters.

Pocahontas

Smith said that Pocahontas
rushed between him and his executioners. She wrapped
her arms around him, and placed her own head against
his. Pocahontas successfully begged her royal father to
spare Smith's life.

The story of brave Pocahontas has become an
American legend. Yet was this truly a last-minute rescue?
Perhaps John Smith was mistaken about this event,
just as he was about why the Powhatan fed him so well.
Wahunsanacock may have only wanted to scare his prisoner.

7

Chief Powhatan might even have decided to make the soldier an ally—an adopted member of his family. In their ceremony for adoption, the Powhatan had a family member pretend to rescue the new relative from death.

In the next years, contact between English colonists and the Powhatan included many misunderstandings about power and property. These problems and others brought enormous changes to the Powhatan's traditional way of life.

8

John Smith may have misunderstood his "rescue" by Pocahontas.

WHO ARE THE POWHATAN?

The Powhatan (pronounced pow-HAT-un) are native peoples of the Middle Atlantic coast. They lived in what is now Virginia and Maryland, in an area about 100 miles (160 kilometers) long and wide.

The Powhatan continue to live in Virginia.

9

This woodland area contained many rivers, streams, and marshes. Waterways even influenced the local peoples' names. In the Algonquian languages they spoke, Powhatan means "waterfall." At one time, between 8,000 and 20,000 people lived in this area. They occupied more than 200 communities.

These people belonged to nearly 30 different tribes. The strong leader named Wahunsonacock, later called Powhatan, had inherited a confederacy of six tribes. These were the Appamatuck, Arrohateck, Mattaponi, Pamunkey, Powhatan, and Youghtanund. In the late 1500s, Wahunsonacock overtook other tribes, which joined his confederacy. He united nearly 30 tribes into the small but powerful nation we now call the Powhatan confederacy. Even though these tribes have their own names, they are often known simply as the Powhatan.

The Powhatan peoples were related to the Delaware or Lenape tribes of what is now New Jersey, Pennsylvania, and New York. Members of the Powhatan confederacy

A carving of Wahunsanacock stands at the Pamunkey Indian Museum.

traded with but often fought neighbor tribes who had different relatives and languages. These enemies included the Susquehannock, Massawomecks and Monacan peoples.

After Europeans arrived in their territory in the 16th century, many Powhatan died from disease and war. By the early 1700s, only about 1,000 Powhatan remained alive.

11

Today, there are between 3,000 and 5,000 Powhatan. Many live in small parts of their traditional territories in Virginia. One Powhatan tribe lives in New Jersey. Other Powhatan live elsewhere along the East Coast.

Many Powhatan live in Virginia and New Jersey.

A MILD CLIMATE

The Powhatan farmed and also fished, hunted, and gathered their food. The mild climate and many resources of their territory helped them. The Powhatan prepared fields for planting by slashing away trees and burning remaining tree stumps. This method left behind ash that helped crops grow. Women and girls

Powhatan speared fish from dugout canoes.

planted and harvested crops including corn, beans, squash, and sunflowers. They also planted tobacco, which was an important part of their religious ceremonies. The Powhatan dried some of their food for winter use. They cooked some right away in tasty stews, combined with fish and shellfish caught by Powhatan men and boys.

13

The shore provided many clams, crabs, and oysters. The Powhatan also ate freshwater fish from the many streams and rivers.

For fishing and hunting, long canoes were an important method of transportation. Over several weeks, Powhatan men carefully and repeatedly burned the centers of cypress trees. They then dug away the burned parts to create canoes. Sometimes, these were 50 feet (15 meters) long. The canoes could carry up to 30 people at a time.

Men hunted waterbirds such as duck and geese. They also used their bows and arrows to hunt wild turkeys. Deer was an important source of meat. Sometimes, Powhatan would wear deerskins to trick and lead deer to a place where many hunters waited. Powhatan men and boys also hunted rabbits and other small animals. Hunting large, dangerous bears, though, was a job only for men.

Women and girls gathered wild plants, roots, nuts, berries, and other fruit. Some was eaten right away while

Indian hunters wore deer capes to trick their prey.

part was stored or dried for later use. They ground nuts as well as corn to use for baking.

Soil along the coast was not good for farming so the Powhatan built permanent homes called yehakin farther inland, near streams or rivers. These locations away from the salt water of the sea also provided fresh water to drink and made canoe travel easier. To avoid floods, the Powhatan built their homes on high ground.

Powhatan women constructed homes by bending young wood into frames. The women then covered the

15

frames with sheets of bark or mats woven from reeds. Yehakin were shaped like rectangles. These longhouses had one large room and were different sizes. Some held only six people, while others could hold 20 or more. On winter hunting trips, women built temporary round shelters. The Powhatan used these for several months. They then returned to their yehakins.

A Powhatan longhouse

"THEY MAKE GOOD CHEER"

Each yehakin was occupied by a Powhatan family that included a father, mother, children, and sometimes grandparents. While a bride moved into her new husband's home, a mother's family was most important. Powhatan inherited belongings and positions of power through their female relatives.

Mothers kept babies snug and safe in cradleboards. Children did not wear clothes until they were eight to 12 years old. The Powhatan believed that in their mild climate this made them healthier and stronger. Bear grease rubbed into their skin kept children warmer and protected from insect bites. Often, Powhatan went barefoot. Women made the leather

A 16th-century drawing of a Native American village

17

A Powhatan girl in traditional dress

moccasins worn in winter and during travel.

Women also sewed the deerskin skirts they wore and the deerskin breechcloths and leggings that men wore. In winter, Powhatan people added leather, fur, or feather capes. Women often decorated clothing with beads. Girls learned these jobs by watching and helping their mothers. Weaving baskets and making clay pots were other skills girls learned. Powhatan women also tattooed themselves in decorative patterns. They rubbed charcoal into scratches to create these designs. This was another part of grown-up life that girls watched with much interest.

Boys learned how to make canoes and how to hunt and fish from their fathers. It was fun learning how to make sounds that would call some animals to them. Boys

Canoes were made from cypress logs.

practiced making wooden bows, arrows, traps and spears. They learned to make arrowheads and knives from stone, shell, bone, and bird beaks. Because longhouses were dark and smoke-filled, much of this everyday work took place in open-sided sheds. These stood next to the yehakins.

The Powhatan played as well as worked. Boys had toy bows and arrows. Both boys and girls enjoyed music, dances, and races. They liked to dress up in beads, adult clothes, and body paint. Ball games and counting games

19

A 1590 engraving of a village and gardens includes a hut at the top right used to scare away birds.

were also popular. Powhatan men liked competing in stickball games, too. Powhatan boys had one chore that could sometimes be fun, as well. As crops grew ripe, a boy would sit in a scarecrow house in the middle of the field. It was his job to make noises to chase away any animals or birds that might try to eat the crop. Sometimes, a boy would stretch his legs by running after some of these pests.

Storytelling was another enjoyable way to spend time and teach children about their world. At special times such as harvests, the whole village feasted and celebrated. One of the first Englishmen to visit the Powhatan, Thomas Hariot, described such a Powhatan celebration with some envy. "They make good cheer together," Hariot wrote. "Yet they are moderate in their eating, whereby they avoid sickness. I would to God we would follow their example."

Villages could be small or large. Some contained a handful of yehakins and sheds while others held more than 20 longhouses and other buildings. Larger villages contained a separate temple. Villages were often surrounded by a high wooden fence called a palisade. Its pointed stakes kept out possible enemies.

Sixteenth-century Native Americans were "moderate" in their eating.

21

VILLAGE AND TRIBE LEADERS

The smallest villages did not have a chief. They obeyed the rules of the chief of the nearest larger village. A Powhatan chief was called a werowance. This position was inherited. If there was no man in the mother's family to inherit it, a woman would become the female chief or werowansqua.

Village werowances received gifts called tribute from the villagers they governed. These gifts might include food, furs, pearls, and copper beads.

Werowances lived in bigger houses, wore fancier clothing, and had more belongings, such as the shell money called wampum that Powhatan used in trade. Powhatan and other native peoples

Wampum beads and shell

22

A line engraving of Chief Powhatan from John Smith's 1624 history book.

often wore decorative wampum belts. A village with its own chief usually had a storage shed to hold tribute. It was often protected by a palisade.

Village werowances themselves obeyed and paid tribute to the leader of the entire tribe. This paramount chief or head werowance made decisions about trade and war. He was the richest, most powerful member of the tribe. Rich and powerful men often had more than one wife. Their families sometimes had servants.

The Powhatan respected bravery. All teenage boys ran a gauntlet and went through dangerous ceremonies before they were

Powhatan warriors and hunters used bows and arrows.

24

considered men. These included living on their own in the woods for several weeks or even months. Boys also had to take unpleasant herb drinks that made them see and hear strange things. These experiences were another test of courage and supposedly helped boys learn more about themselves and the spirit world. Brave, wise warriors who survived into old age became village leaders, too. They gave advice during times of war. These respected councilors were also wealthy.

Other village leaders included healers and priests called kwiocos. Powhatan respected these people for their practical knowledge and their knowledge of the spirit world. Village kwiocos themselves listened to and believed the kwioco who advised the head werowance. The temple in this paramount chief's village was larger and grander than others.

THE SPIRIT WORLD

The Powhatan believed in many gods. Powhatan tribes had different stories about the god who created the world. One tribe believed that this chief god took the shape of a Great Hare. He fought with wind gods when he created the first people.

The Powhatan believed that forces in nature, such as lightning and fire, had their own gods. Many Powhatan worshipped the sun. The Powhatan offered bits of their sacred plant, tobacco, to these gods when they prayed. Powhatan also respected the spirits they believed

The Powhatan believed lightning had its own god.

Wooden statues surrounding a dance circle have human faces.

lived in trees, fields, and rivers. They thanked them for good harvests and hunting. They taught their children to honor the spirits and gods.

In their temples and outdoors, Powhatan kept wooden statues of their gods. Because Powhatan believed

27

the gods sometimes took human shape, these statues had human faces. The kwiocos prayed and led ceremonies near these statues. People left offerings there. The kwiocos also held ceremonies in sweat lodges to help people become pure. Some villages had special burial houses for their dead. The Powhatan believed in a life after death. Belongings to be used in the afterlife were often placed alongside the dead person.

The Powhatan believed that their priests could see into the future. Because his kwiocos warned Wahunsonacock about people from the East, he declared war on an eastern tribe. Yet it was actually the arrival of European explorers and colonists that seemed to make this prophecy true.

A STRONG NATION ENDS

In the 1570s, Spanish explorers were the first Europeans to meet the Powhatan. These explorers fought the Powhatan and even kidnapped one young man. In the

English settlers build a fort at Jamestown in 1607.

29

1580s, English colonists settled just south of Powhatan territory. In 1607, however, the English established Jamestown. This colony was right in the center of the Powhatan confederacy. It was the beginning of the end of this strong nation.

Wahunsonacock felt uneasy about Jamestown. He hoped to trade for English weapons to fight traditional enemies. Yet he did not know how dangerous the colonists might be. Conflicts broke out between the Powhatan and English. In late 1607, the Powhatan captured Captain John Smith. This is when Wahunsonacock's daughter Matoaka supposedly rescued Smith from death. The English knew her by her nickname of Pocahontas, which means playful. The young girl later visited Jamestown several times.

Between 1609 and 1614, some fighting continued. On one of her visits to the colony, Pocahontas was held prisoner. She became a Christian and was given the new name of Rebecca. Peace came in 1614 when Pocahontas married

Pocahontas married John Rolfe in 1614.

colonist John Rolfe. A widower, Rolfe explained in a letter to the colony's governor that he wanted to marry the young Powhatan woman "for the good of this [colony], for the honor of our country, [and] for the glory of God." Yet Rolfe also admitted he had deep feelings for her, writing that she had had his "best thoughts ... for a long time."

31

The couple had a child and traveled to England. The young mother died there of illness in 1617. As John Rolfe later wrote in a letter, Pocahontas tried to comfort her sad husband just before she died, saying "All must die. 'Tis enough that the

Pocahontas and her son, Thomas

child lives." Their son, Thomas, was then just 2 years old. Eight months after he received the news of his favorite daughter's death, Wahunsonacock died.

In Virginia, a long, bloody war began in 1622, when Wahunsonacock's brother Opechancanough became paramount chief. For 10 years, the English burned Powhatan homes and crops and killed women and children. Powhatan warriors killed many colonists, but more arrived. By 1632, the Powhatan confederacy was

Chief Opechancanough fought a losing battle against the colonists.

greatly weakened. Still, in 1644, the elderly Opechancanough again declared war, which the Powhatan
eventually lost.

Between 1646 and 1651, the Powhatan signed
treaties that limited their territory and freedom. Many

The settlement of Jamestown forever changed the Powhatan way of life.

Powhatan had died in the wars. The surviving Powhatan agreed to pay a seasonal tribute to the English king. They would send "20 beaver skins at the going away of geese yearly." They would also live on small reservations inside their traditional lands. The Powhatan's existence as a strong, independent confederacy was over.

CHANGING AND SURVIVING

Another treaty in 1677 took more land away from Powhatan reservations. By the early 1700s, some member tribes of the confederacy became extinct.

By 1800, very few Powhatan spoke their own languages. Within the next generations, these languages died out. Though some traditional ways remained, the Powhatan adopted Christianity and began new traditions. In 1865, people on the Pamunkey Reservation in Virginia

Pawmunkey Indian Baptist Church was established in 1865.

joined the Indian Baptist Church there. It remains an active church today.

In the late 1800s, the Rappahonack and Nanticoke peoples moved to New Jersey. They invited other Powhatan and native peoples to join them. This community grew into the Powhatan Renape Nation. Renape means "human being" in Algonquian languages. This nation exists today.

In the 19th and 20th centuries, Powhatan in Virginia struggled for another reason. Laws and people there often discriminated against African-Americans. Sometimes these laws affected native peoples, too. When Powhatan sent their children to public schools, used public transportation, or joined the Army, they faced the discrimination that was already there in these organizations.

In the 1920s, some Powhatan people worked to gain more rights. The Pamunkey and Mattaponi peoples established themselves by state law as separate,

A tribal cotton field is next to the Pawmunkey Indian Museum.

organized groups. The Powhatan began participating in powwows and other gatherings that strengthened their traditions and taught others about them.

THE POWHATAN TODAY

Today, Powhatan peoples are successfully working to make their tribes stronger and help themselves. In 1980, their efforts led New Jersey to officially recognize the Powhatan Renape Indian Nation as a tribe. In 1982, the Renape succeeded in getting land from New Jersey for their Rankokus Indian Reservation. The Renape provide help with housing and health matters to tribe members and other native peoples. They have established a museum and hold large, yearly arts festivals. These activities strengthen Powhatan traditions and teach others about them.

A traditional dancer performs at a Renape arts festival.

38

Mary Wade of the Virginia Council of Indians holds a T-shirt listing tribal names as her group seeks federal recognition for the Virginia tribes.

Between 1983 and 1985, Powhatan efforts led
Virginia to officially recognize seven tribes there. These
are the Chickahominy, Eastern Chickahominy, Mattaponi,
Nansemond, Pamunkey, Rappahannock, and Upper
Mattaponi tribes. Every four years, each tribe elects a chief
and council to enforce its laws. Council members also
manage business matters for each tribe.

39

The Mattaponi and Pamunkey run state fisheries on their reservations. The Pamunkey also make and sell many traditional clay pots and other items.

The Mattaponi have set up a shad fish hatchery. Shad is a diet staple and at the center of their culture.

Today, Powhatan peoples in Virginia continue to farm, hunt, and fish on part of their traditional lands. Yet some also work in different jobs outside these reservations. Most Powhatan peoples in Virginia belong to the Baptist or Methodist faiths.

Powhatan children today attend school and learn the subjects taught throughout the United States. Yet the efforts of tribe members also make it possible for Powhatan children and others to learn about Powhatan traditions. The Powhatan look toward the future with pride and hope. This is why the Powhatan Renape Nation has included a rainbow on its flag. Renape Chief Roy Crazy Horse explains that "the rainbow is a

A Chickahominy fancy dancer

symbol of hope, the future, the beauty of the world, and the realization of our highest dreams." Powhatan people expect that their beliefs and efforts will benefit future generations.

41

GLOSSARY

ally—people or countries who agree to help each other in times of trouble

breechcloths—short clothes that wrap around the lower part of someone's body

confederacy—a group that works together and has the same main leader

discriminated—treated people unfairly because of their race, religion, sex, or age

extinct— no longer existing

gauntlet—a double row of people who by tradition hit or yell at the person running down the middle of the row

paramount—the main or most important person, thing, or idea

prophecy—something that a person says will happen in the future

reservation—a large area of land set aside for Native Americans

sweat lodge—building in which heat caused the occupants to perspire to purify the body and spirit

42

DID YOU KNOW?

- The Pamunkey, Mattaponi, and Rappahannock Rivers in Virginia are named for three member tribes of the Powhatan confederacy.

- The words *raccoon* and *opossum* come from the Powhatan language. Colonists adopted the Powhatan words for these animals.

- Some stories about Pocahontas are wrong. She never had a romance with John Smith. When he came to Jamestown, Pocahontas was only 10 or 11 years old.

- In the 19th century, Pocahontas was a popular name given to female racehorses.

- The Powhatan people valued copper as much as the English and other Europeans valued gold.

- During his long lifetime, Chief Powhatan supposedly had 100 wives.

- The Powhatan reservation created by a 1651 treaty was the first reservation in North America.

IMPORTANT DATES

Timeline

1500s	Powhatan confederacy forms and grows.
1580s	English colonists settle just south of Powhatan territory.
1607	English colonists establish Jamestown inside Powhatan territory; Pocahontas supposedly rescues Captain John Smith.
1609	First English-Powhatan War begins; it lasts until 1614.
1614	Pocahontas and John Rolfe marry; she dies in 1617.
1622	Powhatan people are at war with the English until 1632.
1646	Powhatan leaders begin to sign treaties with England that establish reservations.
1920s	Pamunkey and Mattaponi organize legally by state law.
1980	New Jersey officially recognizes the Powhatan Renape Indian Nation as a tribe.
1983	Virginia starts the official recognition of seven Powhatan tribes; this is completed in 1985.

IMPORTANT PEOPLE

MATOAKA (POCAHONTAS) (1595–1617)

Powhatan princess who supposedly rescued Captain John Smith and later married John Rolfe; she was the daughter of Wahunsonacock

OPECHANCANOUGH (1554–1644)

Powhatan chief who led the confederacy after his brother Wahunsonacock died

JOHN ROLFE (1585–1622)

English colonist and successful tobacco planter who married Pocahontas after she became a Christian

CAPTAIN JOHN SMITH (1580–1631)

English soldier who worked for and defended the colonists at Jamestown

WAHUNSONACOCK (POWHATAN) (1545–1618)

Paramount chief who made the Powhatan confederacy larger and ruled when English colonists arrived in Virginia and later settled in Jamestown; he was the father of Pocahontas

WANT TO KNOW MORE?

At the Library

Bial, Raymond. *The Powhatan.* New York: Benchmark/Marshall
　　Cavendish, 2002.

Bruchac, Joseph. *Pocahontas.* San Diego: Silver Whistle Press, 2003

Knight, James. *Jamestown.* New York: Scholastic, 2004.

Sullivan, George. *Pocahontas.* New York: Scholastic, 2002.

On the Web

For more information on the *Powhatan*, use FactHound to track down Web

sites related to this book.

1. Go to *www.facthound.com*

2. Type in a search word related to this book or
　　this book ID: 0756508444.

3. Click on the *Fetch It* button.

Your trusty FactHound will fetch the best Web sites for you!

On the Road

**The Powhatan Renape Nation's
American Indian Heritage Museum**
Box 225
Rancocas, NJ 08073
609/261-4747
To see Powhatan tools and other
items and an outdoor re-creation of
a traditional woodland village

Jamestown Settlement
1367 Colonial Parkway
Jamestown, VA 23081
757/229-4997
To see a re-creation of the
Jamestown fort, the three ships that
carried colonists to Jamestown, and
a re-created Powhatan village

Look for more We the People books about this era:

The Alamo

The Arapaho and Their History

The Battle of the Little Bighorn

The Buffalo Soldiers

The California Gold Rush

The Chumash and Their History

The Creek and Their History

The Erie Canal

Great Women of the Old West

The Lewis and Clark Expedition

The Louisiana Purchase

The Mexican War

The Ojibwe and Their History

The Oregon Trail

The Pony Express

The Santa Fe Trail

The Transcontinental Railroad

The Trail of Tears

The Wampanoag and Their History

The War of 1812

A complete list of We the People titles is available on our Web site:
www.compasspointbooks.com

INDEX

About the Author

Natalie M. Rosinsky writes about history, social studies, economics, science, and other fun things. One of her two cats usually sits on her computer as she works in Mankato, Minnesota. Natalie earned graduate degrees from the University of Wisconsin and has been a high school and college teacher.